THE Seven *Spiritual* CAUSES —— OF —— *Ill* Health

by Rev. Hanna Kroeger, Ms.D

Copyright 1988
by
Hanna Kroeger Publications

2nd Printing 1997

ISBN 1-883713-00-5

TABLE OF CONTENTS

Who supplies another with a constructive thought, has enriched him forever.

—*Alfred A. Montipert*

I dedicate this book to my daughter Anneliese Irmela Kroeger. She opened for me door after door that finally I understood the spriritual need of my fellow man.

Introduction

> Don't walk in front of me
> I may not follow
> Don't walk behind me
> I may not lead
> Walk beside me
> And just be my friend

This book deals with the seven spiritual causes of illnesses. You can do this at home, you can undo the knots which tie you to a certain illness, which tie you to an unbalanced condition which is illness. You will be free. It is the truth that will make you free.

Emanuel Golden, M.D. writes:

Good health is your responsibility. Most Americans view doctors as omnipotent persons who know all there is to know about health. Thus, when one's health fails, the immediate blame falls upon the medical community. This is especially true where a disease is discovered several months after it has begun decaying the body.

Your physician is only able to do for you what you let him do. He cannot read your mind, feel your pains or guess at your problems. When you hear a rattle in your car, or feel it is losing power, you see to its causes immediately. Similarly, if you begin feeling below par, notice a symptom that does not disappear or feel pain in various parts of your body, you should not wait until you can't walk to have it diagnosed. Have it checked immediately. You are ultimately responsible for your own good health!

Prevention of illness is almost totally up to you. Preventing illness is not only easier and less costly (in both time and money) than curing them, but prevention also help you live longer. Every time you get sick, you age. This is true even if the cure is quick and simple. There are many things with which you can fortify your body's natural immunity system to ward off disease, slow down degenerative processes and keep you healthier.

CHAPTER I

Spiritual
Neglect
As A
Cause of Ill Health

Will power alone
makes chaos;
realization alone is dead.
Combine both
and you have a powerful
creative flame from
the universe.

Spiritual Neglect

For many people, this is a new thought, a new idea. I will talk about this a little bit, so you can help yourself to better health.

Our body is a miracle in itself. Without our conscious knowing, many functions take place. Day and night, the heart beats. Day and night, our cells are detoxified and nourished. Day and night, our body works without our conscious efforts. "Why then," you say "should I do anything about it? Why should I work on the subject neglect when all runs smoothly without my efforts?"

All of us want to be perfect in body, mind and spirit. Therefore, we have to look at the subject "neglect" not only in the physical. See my book "God Helps Those Who Help Themselves." It is discussed at lengths there. We have to examine this in a different way. Mental and spiritual health is needed to keep the different functions of the body running. An average driver of a motorcar is usually sensitive to the needs of its engine but often very insensitive to the requirements of his/her own body.

We ignore our warning signs, one after another. We sail through one red light after another, until one day we wake up and say, "Hey, what am I doing?"

In some instances it is too late, others can be repaired. Let us be steady and hear and treat the natural God given path.

The Pituitary Gland

The pituitary gland is your master gland which controls the complex functions of your body.

The pituitary gland is located in the middle of the head. The output of the pituitary hormones control:

(a) the chemical balance
(b) the nerve impulses from the neighboring part of the brain called hypothalamus
(c) the endocrine system and their secretion of hormones and enzymes.

This tiny gland with its surrounding, controls the heartbeat, blood pressure, temperature and the functions of the body which are not subject to conscious awareness. This pituitary gland with hypothalamus is the go-between of intellect-emotion and body functions.

Whatever happens to the body, this center we call X is notified at once through the nerve fibers and impulse actions. ALSO, in reverse, any thought process from the brain will go into the body through center X. This is the explanation of "Heal Yourself." This is the explanation that by neglecting positive thought form, the body functions in all departments will suffer. Therefore, by changing the thought pattern from disease to wellness, from dying to health, every department of the body is favorably changed. Many of us have lost the ability to communicate between mind, emotions and body.

The switch is the pituitary gland. In case of neglect, the pituitary gland becomes lazy. Or it may be overstimulated, as in convulsive disorders, when the entire nervous system goes into contraction and with it every muscle in the body.

Spiritual neglect causes tightening of the muscles and stiffness of joints and tendons. As children, we were taught rhymes, little verses, songs and verses from the Bible. When in school, learning by heart of songs and verses is not practiced any longer. Singing in groups, such as folk songs, happens seldom. To "sing along" is replaced by radio and television. We are robbed of one great tool: singing, reciting and expressing ourselves. This is the healing in churches that people sing together, that the disciple Thomas, and the disciple Matthew, are coming together through the songs that are offered to God that His will not mine shall be done. Many healings are reported in all churches and it is this fact that they sing together. The tool most neglected should be practiced.

The human mind has far more potential than we ever dreamed possible. There is almost nothing that our brains are incapable of. Scientists tell us that we use, at most, only ten percent of our brainpower.

Have you ever wondered how much you could improve your life if only you could unleash the power of your mind? You can. This chapter will help you and will give you keys to open the door for understanding. Thoughts and will power go together; even in the brain they have their seats side by side. They are brothers like two disciples of Jesus were brothers.

The Will To Live

In my opinion, neglect of mind and the creative force within are undoubtedly the most important factors of life.

Spiritual neglect is widespread. On the physical level it expresses itself in the following:

- confusion
- mental problems
- stiff muscles
- stiff joints
- congested digestive tract
- deafness
- muscle tension
- tension in the heart muscle

For centuries religious organizations advocated fasting at certain times of the year as before Easter, when some foods are cut out from the diet. In the Islamic religion, during the Moslem month Ramadan, food and fluid cannot be consumed from sunrise to sunset. Very, very difficult to do in the summertime when the sun scorches the barren hills and the trodden empty road.

Why was fasting always a part of strong religions? It is a quest for inner purity. It is a heart's desire to partake in clear, sparkling, pulsating red blood. There is no denying that the human body should periodically undergo a purifying fast.

One of the most rewarding fasts came from the American Indians, the Seneca Indian Cleansing Diet. It is amazing how light you feel. It is amazing how pure your thoughts become. And there is no hardship in doing the amazing American Indian purification diet.

Prolonged purification fasts have disadvantages; such are that the precious alkaline minerals are lost. The person's fasting body will draw on all the alkaline minerals stored away in the bones and elsewhere, such as calcium, magnesium, potassium, zinc and others. We cannot allow the loss of these minerals. A water fast for several weeks brings trouble in that atomic poisons, fallout, pesticides and chemicals are stored in the fatty tissue and by water fasting they are released into the blood system and lymph system and end up in bone marrow, the last place you want the poisons.

For spiritual purification, the named Seneca Indian Cleansing Diet, as well as the following diet, are good. You do not have to become a monk or a follower of a guru to pursue your inner desire for spiritual balance. Obtain your balance by singing, humming, reciting a poem, by laughing at little things. Obtain your balance by walking through your garden, your nearest park, feel the leaves, smell the flowers. Pick an apple from a tree. The tree gives you the apple with joy; take it and enjoy it. Feel that you are a precious being of this earth, know that you are a child of God. And with this you build a stronghold, you build balance.

In particular, problems of muscle tensions, constrictions (stomach), mental illness and troubles of all kinds have a great deal to do with spiritual neglect. "You cannot stomach something" is an expression used in our daily language. Your realization, your inner tuition, your glimpse into the tremendous work of all surrounding forces of God of Goodness has to have a counterpart that this inner awareness can be made manifest on this earth. This counterpart is your will. It is Matthew, the disciple of Christ, the brother of Thomas. It is through will that the teachings of realization become "objectivated," as Schopenhauer said. Through the power of will and the inner understanding, things can be manifested.

What Can We Do?

Fasting For Spiritual Reasons

The short cuts to fasting for spiritual reasons are the following approved methods. They are very, very effective.

Take 1 pound manukka raisins and soak them in 4 quarts water, distilled preferred, for

24 hours. Stir frequently and drink 1 to 1½ quarts of the water in small sips in the morning from 7 a.m. to 11 a.m., or 8 a.m. to noon. For 1 hour take neither food nor drink, and have lunch consisting of vegetable and salad and fish or eggs or cheese. The supper is your choice of food but should not be taken later than 6 p.m. Do this for 2 to 4 weeks, or as you feel it is necessary. Meditate short periods, 5 to 10 minutes, several times a day. It is not the length, it is the depth that counts for us Westerners.

You may also use 36 ounces of grape juice in the above described manner; however, you have to add 6 ounces of water to the 36 ounces of grape juice in order for it to work. Why? I don't know. It must be a secret of the electromagnetic field which we do not know too much about.

Seneca Indian Cleansing Diet

This diet was contributed by the Seneca Indians.

First day: Eat only fruit and all you want. Try apples, berries, watermelon, pears, peaches, cherries, whole citrus fruit and so forth. No bananas.

Second day: Drink all the herb teas you want, such as raspberry, hyssop, chamomile or peppermint. You may sweeten the tea slightly with honey or maple sugar.

Third day: Eat all vegetables you want. Have them raw, steamed or both.

Fourth day: Make a big pot of vegetable broth by boiling cauliflower, cabbage, onion, green pepper, parsley or whatever you have available. Season with sea salt or vegetable broth cubes. Drink this rich mineral broth all day long.

This diet has the following effect. The first day the colon is cleansed (your wastebasket). The second day you release toxins, salt and excessive calcium deposits in the muscles, tissue and organs. The third day the digestive tract is supplied with healthful, mineral rich bulk. On the fourth day the blood, lymph and inner organs are mineralized. That makes a lot of sense!

Here are Remedies You Like to Hear About

The weapon to counteract spiritual neglect is will power. Will power to change your present situation, will power to live, will power to start and/or to finish the job God gave you to do. Your heart gives you direction in life. You promised God to do a certain job such as uplift someone, preach, teach, help, invent, write a book.

You say "Next week I will start." Next week comes and you postpone your work for a month, then several months, then a year and what happens? Your joints start hurting, your period becomes painful and crampy, your heart acts up, your strength goes down. Now analyze your situation thoroughly. Take the power of understanding, which is closely connected with your will power and look at your situation squarely in the eyes. Where did I fail? What did the little voice in my heart say? Where should I start? What does God want me to do? Did I fail to give thanks? Did I fail to forgive and did I fail to give? After you employed the power of understanding, change your desperate situation with your power of the will.

Happy people generally don't get sick. They have so much to laugh at; they have so many people to laugh with. Look at our teen-agers. Ask them for the reason of their laughter. It is a little thing like a cat or another animal, a funny outlandish hair style. They laugh about an apple in the tree which they cannot shake down.

At my summer retreat, I employ teen-agers. We have so much fun and the food served has such happy vibrations. Guests always say, "Your food is sooo good." It may be a simple pea soup. The teen-ager stirs twenty times in the soup, every time saying, "I hope it is good," or "I wish the guests like my soup," and they laugh. By creating fantastic salads with joy and by preparing wonderful cakes with more whipped cream than is needed, they create a vibration of happiness and laughter and our guests drink and eat the happiness.

Laugh at little things and at big ones to get your pituitary gland going. Do not forget to laugh.

It is contagious.

It is uplifting.

It is healing.

I was once called to the deathbed of a dear friend. I learned the 23rd psalm by heart. I wanted to help her. I asked a minister to give me the most suited passages from the Bible. Thus equipped, I visited her. After a while, the friend asked, "Why does the Lord not take me?" "Oh Honey," I said, "they are just sweeping the floors and whitewashing the walls for you." She started to laugh and the abscess in her lung burst. She spit up terrible stuff between tears and laughter. She was healed. Laughter heals the lungs and endocrine system.

People who are at peace with themselves and at peace with their surroundings are not very likely to get sick.

I personally know how difficult it is to be at peace with oneself and one's surroundings. Whenever I have trouble that way, I ask our Lord for help. I ask for guidance and strength so I can shift back to peace.

Here are helping tools which you may employ:

- Look for a meditation group
- Look for a yoga teacher

By employing slow movements of the body, you achieve the needed balance.

Take a long walk. Look at the trees, the flowers, watch

the birds, the creeping creatures at your feet and all the magnificent creations of God. You will bounce back to peace, the natural state of your being. Being in balance your flu will be gone and the troubles with your eyes which had been aching, watering or not focusing are a lot, lot better.

Don't forget to be thankful. Thankfulness is the expression of your soul. Thankfulness is the language of your soul. True thankfulness is rare. Even our Lord Jesus had to say a word about it. When someone is made whole "Healed" and gives thanks, it is a seal, it is a covering, it is a protective veil that no other imperfection can get a hold of them. That no other disease can destroy them. They have sealed the body against all negations.

When someone sends a thank-you note, I rejoice, for I know this person *stays healed,* stays well. Thank-you notes for Christmas are a request of your soul to give thanks to God and your beloved ones and your fellow man. Give thanks to the indwelling goodness of your fellow men. Also, by writing the cards, you straighten out your neglected self, your selfishness, and by doing so, you make yourself whole. People who have a purpose in life seldom get sick.

This is one of the most important duties as we come into retirement age. We have to seek out a true purpose in life.

Maybe you have the tremendous good fortune to watch over your little grandchildren while your daughter goes to work. You don't have time to be sick. The little one cries for the bottle and to be diapered. The older one has to be dressed and combed and the school children have to be guided to become good citizens. They have to learn from you and your experiences in life. What a wonderful time you have. What a fortunate person you are.

Father is equally needed. No one has time to repair the faucets, no one takes time to repair the shed or repair whatever is needed. Grandfathers are the most useful creations that God ever invented. He teaches the slow learners in school, he repairs the toys and roller skates and keeps the happiness in the families.

In case you do not belong to those lucky ones that can help the grandchildren to grow up, there are many, many places you can help. There are many who need your guidance, your help, your reassurance, your love and your life experiences in this world. While doing it selflessly, you are staying well because the angels of the Lord have the order to be with you always.

A newspaper reporter had been assigned to do a story on an unusual inner city church project. A young doctor, in gratitude to God, had decided to give two years of his life ministering to people in need. With the church's help, he established a health clinic in the inner city. The volunteer staff included two nurses who had decided to join the doctor in his ministry of service. The reporter doing the story was in the clinic one night when a man was wheeled in on a stretcher. The man was a skid row alcoholic.

He was dirty and his body gave off an unbearable stench. The man had suffered a very serious leg injury which had gone untreated and the infection contributed to the terrible smell. One of the nurses immediately knelt beside the stretcher. She began cleaning the man's wound, getting him ready for the doctor to examine. The reporter watched the nurse for a few seconds. It was all he could stand. He began to feel sick and, as he turned away to leave the room, he said to the nurse, "I wouldn't do that for a million dollars!" And the young nurse replied quietly, "Neither would *I!*"

Another Tool to Harmony Is Breathing

When we breathe in we are closer to God, to the universal presence. As we breathe in we are receiving strength. As we breathe out, as we exhale, we are releasing old stuff which we do not need. As we breathe in, we should imagine a soft color such as pink, blue or green. As we exhale, we should exhale used up energies in darker colors. This will not only oxygenate your blood, but it will also spiritualize your being. Blood is the carrier of energies. Purified energies carry in with your breath and uplift your mind and soul.

Energy Breath

(suck air in)   Think "IN"
(push air out)   Think "OUT"

(suck air in)   Think "IN"
(push air out)   Think "OUT"
(suck air in)   Think "IN"
(push air out)   Think "OUT"
(push air out)   Think "OUT"
(push air out)   Think "OUT"

Repeat a few times. You should feel energized.

Health practitioners always point out how important breathing is. Breathe out, breathe in. It oxygenates the body. It helps every cell.

When it comes to techniques in spiritual neglect, breathing becomes vital. You need rhythm because the universe is rhythm. A person breathing in rhythm is always more positive, more creative. So you use that knowledge and breathe in rhythm. Look at our earth. She is breathing in rhythm. Ebb and tide are the breath of this earth. If we disturb this by atomic explosion, even ebb and tide come out of rhythm. So, it is also important for us. If we watch our breathing, we will find that most of us breathe without reason or rhythm. But this is important; the rhythm in breathing causes all of the molecules in the body to take the same direction.

CHAPTER II

Spiritual Trauma

Trauma as a Cause of Ill Health

A Smile

A smile costs nothing, but gives much. It enriches those who receive; without making poorer those who give. It takes but a moment, but the memory of it sometimes lasts forever. None is so rich or mighty that he can get along without it, and none is so poor but that he can be made rich by it. A smile creates happiness in the home, fosters good will in business, and is the countersign of friendship. It brings rest to the weary, cheer to the discouraged, sunshine to the sad, and it is nature's best antidote for trouble. Yet it cannot be bought, begged, borrowed, or stolen, for it is something that is of no value to anyone until it is given away. Some people are too tired to give you a smile. Give them one of yours, as none needs a smile so much as he who has no more to give.

—*Author unknown*

Spiritual Trauma

Trauma is an injury. It can be an accident or an operation. An accident usually has a deeper injury because through a blow or a broken bone, it becomes more difficult to heal. There is pressure, there are injured capillaries, there can be deep blood clots, congestion, bruises and tears. In an operation, skillfully these injuries are avoided and the repair is done, without bruised tissue, without jarred nerves. When trauma is of long standing, the injury can press on other parts of the body. It is important to heal sores completely and eliminate scars if at all possible.

The same happens on the mental and spiritual level. If there is an injury, it has to be healed completely. Otherwise a person never will be that jewel Our Creator intended to make.

A deep feeling of guilt wants to come to our face. We have arguments. Why did I have an accident? Why did I shout? Why did I slide? Why was I nasty?

In life, you can come "off the road," you "lose control," you "cannot stop," you're "thrown around." All these are accidents. In court they say "I did not see him coming." It is time that you inspect your life and see where you are and where you are going.

THERE ARE TWO KINDS OF SPIRITUAL TRAUMA

There are two kinds of spiritual trauma. One is the programming of the fetus and the child up until the seventh year. They have to be deprogrammed with outside help. The other is trauma by hypnotizing and conditioning the brain and emotions. The latter makes a neurological obstruction and carries on for a long, long time or until the individual does something about it. To remove this kind of obstruction is up to the individual.

Prenatal Influences

The only time parents are in complete charge of the nature of the child are the wonderful nine months before birth. The fetus feels the emotions of the parents also. It appears to hear the words spoken by the parents. During these formative months, lots of good things can influence the coming child. Some parents want their child to take up a special trait in its later years and by talking frequently about it, they accomplish just that. It is reported that the child later on picks up the profession the parents wanted the child to have. When parents sing a lot, the baby picks it up and becomes a happy, singing child. Now the same thing also goes to the negative side.

If a child is not wanted or even an abortion attempt is made, this child becomes suicidal and depressed. I call it conditioned. There are many grown-ups who can retrace their negativity to these events and also to the tender years up to the age of three.

A psychologist wrote: "I found the people trying to commit suicide do this every year on the precise date. While probing into these phenomena he found that this was that special time the parents wanted to abort the baby."

A child in the formative years up to three years, some for longer, can be programmed in many ways. Particularly thoughts and words of hate, thoughts and words of destructive nature, thoughts and words of fear, can program a fetus for life.

I teach my young mothers to sing and praise, surround yourself with good music. Dr. Chavez, a conductor of music at the University of Texas, told me that they made extensive studies of this nature at the University of Mexico City. They found that in every case when a mother was surrounded by good music the child was much brighter, more loving, more giving. They found that children subjected in the formative years to tenderness in music became ripe for college, teaching at the age of fifteen. Rock music, he concluded, made dull, incoherent, demanding children and many became drug addicts already in Senior High School.

Here is an example of traumatic-emotional experiences.

A small three year old boy was taken shopping in a big department store with his mother. All at once, he found himself all alone. He had wandered around the toy display and could not find his mother. She was looking for him but searched in the wrong direction.

That tremendous shock of being alone carried over until he was 17 years of age, when he came to me for an acne problem. His acne was unmanageable and also he could not manage his life. A deep fear overshadowed everything. He was thin, far too thin, had bald spots, restless hands as if he had taken dope, his skin was gray, he could hardly keep up with school, felt depressed to the extent of suicide.

"You are in shock," I said. "What happened, did your mother die?" "I am fine," he answered. Tell me what it is," I insisted. "You are in shock for many years. Think back." He closed his eyes and through the closed eyes, tears dropped down one by one. I let him cry for a while, and then I said, "This is enough, tell it." Reluctantly, he told the story when he was lost in a department store 15 years ago. These ten minutes, more or less, of total despair had damaged this young man's health for 15 years. Ten minutes is a long time for an emotional and sensitive person.

Trauma

Trauma can be a spiritual cause of ill health. Trauma can go back to the time before you are born.

Here comes the tragedy of the unwanted child, the unloved. Unloved by the parents because of a burden, unloved by the grandparents, unloved by brothers and sisters because he/she is the last of the family, somewhat slow or they are jealous. In any case, children carry this cross with them all their lives. Only a few make it under these dramatic circumstances. They cannot become whole; they are split apart. I call them the programmed children.

Here I am reporting the discovery of a clinical psychotherapist, Dr. Andrew Feldman of Canada. This gentleman discovered an incredible link between suicide attempts and attempted abortion and he said there is good evidence that embryos remember what happened to them in the womb.

It is interesting to know that Dr. Andrew Feldman observed that suicide attempts are usually made in the months and date of the year when their mothers attempted abortion. Memory is not just in the brain, the psychologist said, it also is in the muscles, connective tissue and bone marrow. Memory seems to be recorded on the cellular level.

PROGRAMMED PEOPLE NEED BIRTHRIGHT TEA.

To break these spells when adults do not even know where it comes from, I suggest a formula of herbs called *Birthright Tea*. It contains rosemary, blue vervain and calamus root. Drink one cup two times a day for fourteen days. This is an amazing formula with most amazing results.

Breaking of bones is a sign that in the physical world we become too rigid because we did not want to change. We became too one-sided in our opinion, too one-sided in our situation, our possession. For example, the mental and spiritual inflexibility expresses itself in breakage of bones. A housewife lived in a comfortable home for 20 years. It was in a suburb of Detroit. She had raised her children in this house, she had planted the trees, she had painted and fixed up the house to her very liking. One day her husband was sent to Santa Monica, California. The company had moved and he had to move also. Mrs. White had walked the stairways hundreds of times, but now she fell down and broke her ankle. The reason was not the stairway, but that she did not want to leave her place.

7 Candle Ceremony

In a quiet hour when no one can disturb you, do the following. On the floor, in a wide circle, place seven candles, put them on silver candleholders or on silver quarter pieces. Ignite the candles. Place your problem in the middle of the circle. The house you have to leave, the child you kept so close, the work you loved. Write it out and if you have a picture put a picture of your problem in the middle. Go backwards around the candles. When you come to the place where you started out, say "I break you from my consciousness. I let you go in the name of the Most High. I am free and so are you." Make a motion like the "L" with your right hand. Go backwards again slowly and feel the tension leaving. Every time you come to the starting point, cut yourself loose. Do this seven times. Sometimes you have to repeat it the next and the next day.

An American Indian taught me when you take a child under seven from the place of birth or from the place you lived, go outside and call the name of the child three times, make a movement of gathering so the aura of the child goes with you and your family. If you do not do it, a baby or a child is sick for a long, long time and no one finds the cause of her/his prolonged illness.

I observed this and I found it true. When this is your child's trouble and you had not called the aura with you, go back to the house you lived in with the child in question and call the aura, the emanation, the etheric thread back to your child. They will be healed.

There is help, and I will mention a few here. Incense is used in many churches. The smoke and the smell help to open the obstruction. The American Indians use smoke sticks. Herbs, such as sage, cedar, juniper branches and lavender, are tightly bound together and then ignited at the tip. This has a most remarkable effect to calm the nerves and open mental and emotional obstruction. Also, the smell of lavender alone is very helpful. Carry it with you in a little bag.

Nowadays, our youth employ incense a lot. However, more knowledge should be given as to when to use it and what kind should be used. Sage incense, for example, removes both emotional pain and physical pain. Here is a list of flowers and herbs that can be used as incense or as a tea or just to be carried with you.

Flowers For Healing

Flowers are messengers of the angels and are symbolic of angelic communication. They have a spiritual ministry and are signatures of the soul. Each flower has its own shape, size, color and tone, and sings in its own vibratory keynote. Each flower family is given its own special work to perform for humanity. Each plant bears deeply within its heart a message to the human family.

Acacia Blossom	Love eternal, love immortal.
Amaranth - Golden	Cup of forgetfulness. Cup of compassion. Eventual recovery of inner wisdom. Undying or immortal.
Anemone	Transformation.
Daffodil	Divine adventure.
Fuchsia	At midnight and at dawn they
(Astral Bells)	chime, summoning angels of mercy to minister to all that grieve and suffer.
Goldenrod	Peace.
Heliotrope	Love of soul for soul.
Jasmine	Divine peace, good will.
Lily	Divine conception of love.
Lily of the Valley	Crown of motherhood.
Mistletoe	Tears of lovers.
Narcissus	Rebirth.
Night-Blooming Cereus	Life immortal.
Pansy	Bridge of transition.
Passion Flower	Flower of love.
Poinsettia	Cosmic birth.
Poppy	Activates the human soul during sleep.
Rose - Pink	Aspiration.
Rose - White	Soul attainment, immortality, inner peace.
Rosemary	Soul remembrance.
Violet - White	Link between incoming ego and mother.
Weeping Willow	Communion of prayers between earth and inner planes.

CHAPTER III

Spiritual
Congestion
As A
Cause of Ill Health

Spiritual Congestion Is Widespread

Spiritual congestion is the cause of many, many illnesses. In the physical, we speak about gallstones or constipation or the plaque in the arteries and we all know that we have to do something to decongest our physical body. So is it with our spiritual body.

Like every art requires knowledge and practice, so does this art of healing require knowledge and practice. When you go to an art class, such as painting or woodcarving, you will be instructed about the materials, such as paint, canvas, wood and chisels. What you create afterwards is the creative spirit which forms and you have the privilege through knowledge and practice to use your hands for creating new facets of the Jewel Spirit, God, divine life force.

When we devote ourselves for the benefit of others, more help is given to us. In fact, so much help that we have to sit down to analyze, categorize and practice what is valuable and what is of lesser help.

Learn to become an instrument of the divine. Learn to become a channel of the light force. The greatest hindrance is *Mister Ego* which always wants to slip in. Mister Ego does not belong here at all. The less you are attached to the process, the better healing will work, because we are not the ones to do the job. This job is done by higher powers and we only give our knowledge, our willingness and our hands to heal our fellow man.

Spiritual congestion is expressed in the physical realm in:

- heart trouble
- low blood pressure
- high blood pressure
- emotional trouble
- paralyzed condition in parts or total
- cramps
- rheumatism
- mental illness
- mental limitations

What is Mainly Congested?

The energy centers. In the East, they are called "chakras." It is like an electrical shortage. The flow of energy is not going through. In the East, much time is spent in meditation to open these centers. God gave to the Eastern brother seven energy centers. He gave to the American Indian eight energy centers. To the Western man Our Lord gave nine energy centers. Below is the picture of the Western man's energy centers.

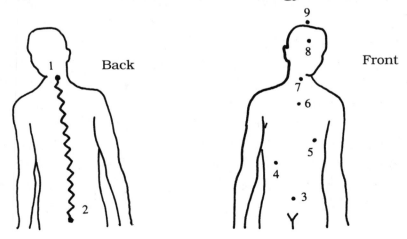

We are checking here the energy centers. These have very, very little to do with anyone's spiritual advancement. Here are some facts you have to know. If the color magenta is low (it is the color over the thymus gland), your immune system is sick. Demand the color magenta back and leave your sodium fluoride from your toothpaste and your sodium fluoride water alone. *Sodium fluoride is the destroyer of the color magenta and of your immune system.* If your color green is too low, or too high, you will have a lot of digestive problems. Demand it be in balance by visualization of the color green and with demand. If your color violet is low, your sugar household is upset and your calcium utilization does not function. Cut down on sweets.

Once I was teaching this truth. A student was constantly falling asleep. She was all dressed in spotless white with a huge white turban on her fair head. I said to myself, "You must be terribly boring." So I told them the funniest story of my life. We had a terrific time. After a while I went back to my subject and she fell asleep again. I asked her if I could check her intake and her output. She agreed. Her intake was ten, but her output was 450 (intake and output have to be alike). I asked her if I could balance her, but she denied and said, "People should know how spiritual I became with my meditation."

Here we have to be more specific. As I pointed out, the current we call aura energy has nine centers in the Western man. These centers act like transformers in an electrical plant. These centers have to be balanced with each other and we have to see to it that they are not congested. One of the tools to balance and clean these centers is colors.

- Color healing is the number one tool to balance the congestion.
- Bach flower remedies is another one.
- Healing with music opens the energy center of the upper torso.
- Crystal healing is another one.
- Touch for health is another one.
- *Reiki* healing is another one.

Our Nine Energy Centers in Color
1. Red
2. Orange
3. Yellow
4. Green
5. Blue
6. Magenta
7. Violet
8. Pink
9. White

What is Reiki?
Reiki (pronounced Ray-Key) is an ancient healing art over 2,500 years old, which was rediscovered in Japan in the nineteenth century. Reiki is a Japanese word meaning "Universal Life Force Energy," the ocean of energy that is all around us. Healing energy is channeled through the practitioner's hands and the

patient is healed not by the Reiki practitioner, but by the Universal Life Force Energy flowing into him or her through the practitioner, who has been "attuned" to such channeling under the guidance of a Reiki Master.

Reiki relieves pain and acute problems quite effectively and is particularly useful in bringing deep relaxation to the patient. Chronic illnesses may require a number of treatments, depending on the nature of the disease. Any sickness which manifests physically is a symptom of disorder on the emotional, mental and spiritual levels. Reiki restores balance and harmony in all these areas, giving a sense of wholeness and well-being. Reiki opens a closed energy center of the aura and emotional body.

Quality of Various Colors

RED   Sensory stimulant, liver energizer, hemoglobin builder, pustulant, stimulates the natural warmth of the body, excitant.

ORANGE   Respiratory stimulant, parathyroid depressant, thyroid stimulant, antispasmodic, carminative, stomachic, lung builder, corrects rickets and soft bones, emetic, mammary stimulant, aromatic.

YELLOW   Motor stimulant, alimentary tract energizer, lymphatic activator, splenic depressant, digestive, cathartic, destroys worms, muscle and nerve stimulant, nerve builder, inspiring, stimulates flow of bile.

LEMON — Cerebral stimulant, thymus activator, antacid, chronic alterative, antiscorbutic, laxative, expectorant, bone builder, loosens all types of congestion.

GREEN — Pituitary stimulant, disinfectant, antiseptic, germicide, muscle and tissue builder, dissolves blood clots, cleanser, detergent, bactericide.

TURQUOISE — Cerebral depressant, acute alterative, combats acidity, skin builder, tonic, relieves pain from sunburn, relieves fever and irritated conditions, cooling and refreshing.

BLUE — Relieves itching, reduces fever, vitality builder, relieves burns, increases perspiration, soothing.

INDIGO — Parathyroid stimulant, thyroid depressant, sedative, respiratory depressant, checks the flow of blood in case of hemorrhage, astringent, relieves pain, arrests discharges, phagocyte builder.

VIOLET   Splenic stimulant, cardiac depressant, lymphatic depressant, motor depressant, builds white corpuscles, muscle and nerve depressant, induces sleep.

PURPLE   Venous stimulant, lowers blood pressure, kidney depressant, adrenal depressant, induces sleep, hypnotic, narcotic, anti-malaria, analgesic, lowers body temperature, decreases pain, decreases sex desire.

MAGENTA   Cardiac energizer, kidney stimulant, emotional equilibrator, aura builder, adrenal stimulant, increases circulation, regulates high and low blood pressure.

SCARLET   Arterial stimulant, heart stimulant, raises blood pressure, kidney stimulant, increases circulation, sex stimulant and builder, adrenal stimulant, venous depressant, stimulates menstruation, increases discharges.

CHAPTER IV

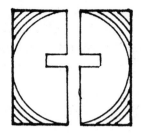

Emotions

Did is a word of achievement.
Won't is a word of retreat.
Might is a word of bereavement.
Can't is a word of defeat.
Ought is a word of duty.
Try is a word each hour.
Will is a word of beauty.
Can is a word of power.

What would our world be without emotions?
Emotions are happiness, joy, freedom, success and true friendship. However, if emotions are disturbed, we speak about sickness, unhappiness, jealousy, hate and all negative powers.

Upset Emotion

Upset emotions can have visible manifestations in the following disease patterns:

- Toxic condition in lymph
- Toxic condition throughout the body
- Skin condition
- Hair loss
- Kidney trouble
- Paralysis
- Metabolic disorders

We have two important glands for decongesting emotions. The first is the pineal gland. This gland is the master gland. It is located close to the pituitary gland, in the middle of the brain, a short distance behind the root of the nose. This gland, when well developed, brings emotional and physical well-being. This gland is also the throne of our faith. As we develop faith, we develop the pineal gland. Faith alone has no power. So God gave us another gland right next to the pineal gland. It is the pituitary gland. The pituitary gland lies in the "Turkish saddle," well embedded, and is the gland of imagination and will.

These two we may call twin glands. Imagine some kind of healing without the power of faith will not bring lasting results. On the other hand, faith, blind faith, without the goal of imaging has no end result and will not open the doors for healing the body. For example: Someone is confined to a wheelchair or bedridden. The first thing this person has to do, and with him all people concerned, is to imagine that he can walk again. See them walking, see them well, see them placing the foot on the floor. And then believe what your mind sees. You cannot tell what comes first, imaging or faith. Both are needed for results.

The first question is, "How can we strengthen these mentioned glands, these power-houses?" The next question is, "How can we line up these glands so they work together?" Here are some suggestions which worked well for me and others.

Chemistry of Emotions

At the National Institute of Mental Health in Bethesda, Maryland, research is under way that could enhance our understanding of the mind/body relationship.

Dr. Candace Pert, Ph.D., chief of the institute section on Brain and Biochemistry, stated "Emotions are not just in the brain but are also in the body and appear to run the immune system, the glands, the intestines. So your whole body is a single-unit integrated circuit, running on biochemicals." Once all of this is fully under-stood, it may provide the medical profession with totally new ways to treat diseases such as cancer, schizophrenia, obesity and AIDS.

Dr. Pert said, "Emotions are not just in the brain but are also in the body and appear to run the immune system." How does the mind exert its effects on the body? By changing one's men-tal attitude from negative to positive and by using relaxation and mental imagery, Dr. Pert believes, one changes the kinds of neuropeptides the body makes. "Changing from the warped neuropeptides that are caused by anger and anxiety to the happy ones actually changes the body chemistry," she said. "You are changing the physical reality of your body as you change your mood."

When Dr. Pert was asked if this dynamic sys-tem might account for reports that when doctors tell a patient he or she has only a short time to live, the white blood cell count immediately drops. In effect, isn't the physician sabotaging the immune system just by giving the progno-sis? "Pessimistic views," she replied, "actually can cause disease. It's like the principle of 'voo-doo death.' You tell people they're going to die, and they die."

"You are changing the physical reality of body as you change your mood."

An emotional crisis does more than injure your psyche. It jeopardizes your physical health. It increases your risk of sickness and even can add to accidental injuries.

Definition of Depression

Physicians and psychiatrists recognize two kinds of depressions.

1. The endogenous form.
2. The neurotic form.

It is recognized that the endogenous form of depression is an imbalance of the chemical structure which, as far as they have discovered, starts in the basal ganglions of the brain stem. There are also basic organic depressions connected with low blood sugar, toxoplasmosis, *Candida albicans* and others.

Researchers of the neurotic forms of depression found that emotional experiences of the past and of the present are ill directed and can cause chemical imbalances which lead to depression.

The first kind of depression is mentioned in my book "God Helps Those Who Help Themselves." The second kind of depression is dealt with in a spiritual way and belays to better understanding of the psychic experiences of the individual involved. These kind of depressed people have to have guidelines. They need a staff to lean on. They need spiritual help. They need Christ. They have to learn to open their eyes to see the beauty of this world and that our Lord can change them from being depressed to being individuals of happiness and success.

In all cases of depression, rub the back of the neck upwards. Apply some *Emu Rub* solution to your fingers and rub it in. Do this two times daily. The herbal solution will penetrate the skin and help your effort to balance the imbalance which can cause depression. I will mention here that depression can be the influence of demonic forces, also. (*See* Chapter VI on demonic influences.)

Rhythm and Its Tremendous Power to Heal Emotions

Rhythm is a tremendous healing factor. The heart heals under the rhythm of 3/4 and the lungs 2/4. The lymphatic system likes an even, soft rhythm like the sound and the rhythm of a brook in the forest.

Rhythm of the heart: every ½ hour give 4 oz of distilled water for 2 days.

Rhythm of the kidney: every 15 minutes give a small piece of watermelon or pear for 3 days.

Rhythm of stomach and colon: every 50 minutes give 2 oz of chlorophyll water for 3 days.

Rhythm of the liver: every 1½ hours give 10 oz limeade for 7 days.

Rhythm of the pancreas: every 45 minutes give 1½ teaspoons paprika in 2 oz pineapple juice (alternate with papaya juice) for 2 days.

Rhythm of the nerves: every 60 minutes give thyme tea and 12 manukka raisins for one week.

Rhythm of the lungs: every 2 hours give 1 cup linden flower tea. Chew 2 small pieces of calamus root on the hour when you do not drink tea. Use it like chewing gum. Spit it out after you chew it. Do this for 3 days.

Enthusiasm

One of the most neglected spiritual powers we have is the power of creative enthusiasm. This power has its seat in the back of the skull in the medulla oblongata. Enthusiasm is connected with daring. It is a special type of power.

In the Middle Ages they called it God's breath. They thought it was the fire of heaven when one was displaying this divine faculty. We all have this spark, but greatly we suppress it. We do not understand that without it we never have the power to discern. We always will be in the mass; we always will be onlookers and not doers.

The television does a terrible job to dull this fire of the Gods. When someone has constant trouble in the neck area, stiff, painful, cannot turn, the power of ingenuity and the power of enthusiasm are not brought to light. These people are always fighters against someone or something, are stiff necked and intolerant.

Without enthusiasm there is no joy in life. Enthusiasm is activated interest. You have to be inspired from life itself, inspired by the Creator and his handy work, inspired by something, and this tremendous power of inspiration is in the base of the skull.

Enthusiasm is electrifying; it is an inward fire. It is God's finger. It is God's divine breath.

A powerful belief is carried by powerful and enthusiastic personalities. Enthusiastic and daring people are quiet about their future dreams. They are steadfast. "The *steadfast* will I make a pillar in the house of my Lord and they shall go out no more." If you lack steadfastness, speak to yourself. Rub the back of your neck and say, "I dare, I dare with the fire of God, I dare."

Here is the sad thing. When people take LSD or other street drugs, the center of enthusiasm is damaged. Also, alcoholism damages this center. Look at people who take drugs. They are numb, without the fire of the Almighty God.

We are children of God. In us is the power of creative enthusiasm. No longer shall it be dormant. We ask, "Oh Lord touch us with your Holy Fire, make us sparkling, make us electrified by you, make us steadfast for you."

When you can say, "I give up drinking, I give up drugs and marijuana," and really do it, you have taken hold of yourself and energy is emanated to heal within. Will, obedience and understanding are the creative powers in your life, in your environment, in your circumstances and in your health.

Prayer Action Plan for Dissolving the Emotional Cause of a Physical Problem

The Hawaiian Kahunas used to get rid of unwanted negative attitudes and feelings by relaxing and commanding these unwanted negative attitudes to leave their bodies while they shook their right and left legs.

I suggest:

1. Review the situation that is presently causing a particular emotional stress.
2. Pick a word that expresses the positive opposite of this negative emotion (example: hate—love; anxiety—security; worry—confidence; impatience—patience, etc.).
3. Place a glass of water next to you.
4. Relax. See yourself beset with the negative emotion. Put it all into the glass of water. Throw water away.
5. Take a fresh cup, preferably porcelain. Fill this cup with water and think that this water contains the necessary solution to your problem—it is filled with the opposite positive emotion. Drink the water, knowing that you are filling yourself with the positive emotion you need, and the negativity will leave you when you next urinate.
6. End session. Then urinate, feeling an exhilaration of positivity.

If you find your trouble in column I, a possible solution could be found in column II.

I		II
Throat	=	Feat
Heart	=	Emotion
Ears	=	Obedience
Eyes	=	Obedience
Fingernail	=	Aggression
Feet	=	Steadfastness
Gallbladder	=	Freedom-power
Knee	=	Submission
Lung	=	Communication
Stomach	=	Feeling
Mouth	=	Acceptance
Muscles	=	Activity
Blood	=	Life force, vitality
Kidney	=	Partnership

CHAPTER V

Karma

In light of our new approaches to sickness, sickness is not to be fought but transmuted. Healing has never taken place by fighting the symptoms. Aspirin removes a headache for a while but the cause of the headache is not touched nor transmuted.

Healing takes place by the transmutation of the cause and by that a person is healed, made whole. Not only that, but a person comes closer to the oneness of their inner being and is transmuted to be made whole.

Concept of Karma

Though the Sanskrit term "karma" is not well-known in the West, it simply means the law of cause and effect, action. This concept is known from the Bible: " ... for whatsoever a man soweth, that shall he also reap." (Galatians 6:7). Broadly viewed, karma means that what we do at any given time affects the outcome of future events. Since this concept is so important to a clear understanding of karmic causes of illness, I will be more specific about this. There are several different types of karma and in order to understand and heal effectively, we must distinguish among them.

There are two major branches of karmic condition which we have to sort out.

The first one is the biggest one. God is law. God has His laws throughout nature, throughout this earth and His universe, for example, the law of gravity. You cannot break the laws of God. You break yourself by not obeying God's laws. If you break a law of God it will return to you in seven: In seven seconds,
seven minutes,
seven hours,
seven days,
seven weeks,
seven months,
seven years.

And in 77 years, when a nation revolts against the laws of God, people will return to the religion of the forefathers or to the new religion of the coming age.

Educative Karma

Too many people have a mistaken idea of karma. They think if they have done certain things, that they are bound thereby. You could have done everything negative in the past, but once you recognize the truth of it and forgive it, you are released from the karma of the past.

Jesus suggested that we use the power of forgiveness in all things. When we finally forgive all past differences and misunderstandings and we walk free from the bondage of karma, it is loosened and we advance accordingly.

Cause and effect is the fourth law we have to discuss, and it is a tremendous contributing factor to understanding health. But again, it is one and only one in fourteen causes of health trouble. Once it is understood, the law of action and reaction is taken away from the obscure, away from the unknown and the terrible attitude. If it is karmic, there is nothing we can do about it.

That we have to discuss thoroughly, and I bring you help.

The average person may not be familiar with the term karma, even though this term has been used for years. It may be because various religious organizations have avoided reference to this. They think it could interfere with the teaching professed. The universe functions with definite laws. Dr. Doreal taught that one cannot break the universal laws, but you break yourself against it.

Jesus made reference to His Father's will and in Matthew 5:17, he states that He came not to destroy the law but to fulfill it. Jesus had great knowledge and power, but He knew that He was not to interfere with the stories told of His temptation by Satan. Matthew 4:1-11 and Luke

4:1-13. What Satan was really up to was testing if Jesus would try to use His power to disobey God's natural laws. Jesus knew that if He would defy the law of gravity by jumping off the pinnacles of the temple, he would disobey His Father's laws. To move about this planet without knowing the laws causes us no end of problems. A karmic condition is not as often found as we think.

Karma is an Eastern word and for us it means unfinished business. An unfinished business with others and with yourself. Karma is not always a carried over condition from past lives as the Easterners state. Karma in this lifetime starts when you promise something and will not do it. As you sow, so you will reap. Forgive 70 times, 70 times. Forgive totally.

Again I say, karma is unfinished business; often times, most often times, we do not know which business it is that is undone. Don't think of an angry God watching for your mistakes. This will all fade in the new knowledge of karma. At the present time, the knowledge coming from the East about karma is paralyzing to most of us. You cannot do anything about it. It is karma.

A young man came to my working place, his feet in sandals, his two toes badly, badly infected. I went to the kitchen to bathe his foot in mild soapy water, whereupon he said, "Just let go, it is karma." I answered, "Karma or not, these toes need help." I bandaged them and he felt better. He came every day, and I washed his feet and applied ointments. After a few days, the foot was healed; he was a young man with lots of healing power in him. "Bob," I said, "after a week you are healed. Where is your karma?" "You took it away. Love took it away," he said and smiled thankfully.

You took it away, yes. That is the answer to karmic condition. Action, action and lots of it. Action talks louder than words, and action is what heals a karmic condition.

Love removes karma.

To have a second chance seems to be the ultimate mark of a compassionate, nonpunishing God, to whom we can relate no matter how good or bad we function. This second chance of birth, life and rebirth is an essential message in the Age of Christ's coming.

When a farmer goes to the field, he does not only sow the seed, he also tends the crop.

He plows the ground
He waters the crop,
He fertilizes it
He removes the thistle,
He waits until it is ripe.

It is action. The work between sowing and harvesting is your job. So karma is action.

There is a second part to the chapter of cause and effect. The chapter of action and reaction, and you, the player, the actor, the director, of your life, you have to know more about it.

The greatest contributing factor of your cause and effect is unkept promises. We go back to Adam and Eve. Adam and Eve ate from the forbidden tree the famous apple, even though they had promised not to do so. And then when God confronted them, Adam said Eve made him eat it, and Eve said "Oh Lord, the snake made me pick the apple and eat it." We still are that way; we blame one another instead of taking responsibility for our own actions. Man thus found that he could ease his conscience and eliminate his sense of guilt by putting the blame on someone else. For centuries, man has put the blame on someone else for his blunder and his lack of motivation. Today many still prefer to close their eyes to their unkept promises and avoid the need to change by putting the blame on God. Of course, not all put the blame on God; men have blamed women, and women have blamed men. Children have blamed their parents, and jobholders their bosses. Others blame the school, the church, the government for holding them back from doing better and keeping their promises. Unkept promises create a tremendous amount of guilt feeling. Guilt feeling is a contributing cause of cancer and unhappiness, even to the point of suicide.

Ignorance Karma

In this category we find suffering caused by our continuing ignorance of important spiritual concepts and cosmic laws. It clearly overlaps educative karma. For example, we might inadvertently take on an unpleasant or dangerous task, accept an accident or sacrifice a pleasure because we have misunderstood what our true natures, powers and duties actually are. Therefore, to avoid this type of unnecessary suffering, we must study, work and develop ourselves so that we do not make mistaken choices from now on. Wisdom erases educative karma.

Bleed-Through Karma

Like ignorance karma, bleed-through karma isn't necessarily based on any sins we might have committed, but, rather, depends on a psychic bleed-through from events of earlier, forgotten periods of this life. Symptoms developed in such earlier situations are re-stimulated by some present time event and begin to manifest in our bodies or our lives. For example, a child had a light accident. She was brought to a physician but nothing showed in x-ray or otherwise. Weeks later, she developed sudden paralysis. This child might be suffering from a bleed-through karma or subliminal memory which had been the crippled, unresolved condition of a previous lifetime. The principle of re-stimulation of forgotten traumas or "misunderstoods" is a very important concept in treating any serious ailment and will be covered again.

This is what Prof. Brauchle showed us. Prof. Brauchle was the head of a 2,000 bed hospital for natural healing in Dresden, Germany in 1937. "In all cases we could suspect karma involvement, try the following. " He taught, "Every night when your child or whoever seems to be afflicted is sleeping, talk to them positively in a low voice. Say, 'I love you, you will be well, all the past is gone, you will be well,' over and over just that much for ten minutes. Next day take another sentence as, 'I love you, I see you walking, I see you jumping, I love you.' Change from night to night for about three to four weeks and the miracle will happen."

Karmic diseases can be people born crippled, born without sight or hearing, but these things also have other causes such as:

Neglect (by parents)
Hypnosis (by parents)
Trauma (by mother)
Miasms (by grandparents)

Too quickly do we associate birth difficulties with karma.

Who suffers more? Is it the child or are the parents the ones that pay karmic debts? Each individual case has to be evaluated and each one has to do it for himself. A crippled child can be a blessing to a family if you let him become a blessing. A crippled child also can be a burden if you let him become a burden. It is up to you. In any and in every case, understanding and forgiveness and love are the keys to all karmic conditions.

It sounds so easy. Believe me, it is not. Every inch of you struggles and struggles hard in sleepless nights and in strenuous days when you search for a solution and an understanding of yourself and your situation.

Old Karmic Pattern

Red clover tops - 5
Burdock root - 7
2 cups a day

Diseases which can be karmic are depression, insanity, susceptibility to infection and being overweight or underweight. In order to overcome these handicaps, do the following thing: *Cut yourself free.*

Ask your favorite person to help. Take a mirror. Slant it slightly on a table. Place your left hand two inches in front of the mirror, palm down.

Ask your dearest friend to sever you from the past. Let him hold your middle and second finger. You and your friend both look into the mirror which symbolizes the past, and your friend says with the power in the name of Jesus, I cut you free from the burden of the past.

Do that up to twelve times in quick succession. I cut you free with the power of Jesus.

What a relief for those who had carried a knapsack on their shoulders for so long.

Jesus came to release us from the past. Therefore, karma is strange to us when we sit and accept it, instead of getting in full swing and releasing it with Jesus' powerful might.

CHAPTER VI

Entities
As A
Cause Of Ill Health

I am now talking about a strange, strange subject. The subject of possessions, obsession of curses, of hexes and voodoo as a cause of human weaknesses and illnesses.

I am fully aware that we live in the 1990s and not in the Middle Ages. I am aware that our time is the time of exact science, that what cannot be proven in the laboratories and under the microscope does not exist for many people. It is now time that we come to grips with this subject and shed truth on it. It is time that we examine it and squarely look into the eyes of something that exists, and yet is unknown and foreign to us.

Is it so unknown? No, it is not! I suppose you read or have read the Bible and again and again you come to a passage of devil possession. Calling out the devil, healing the sick and obsessed, the lunatic and those in trouble. Jesus did it; why do we think that this subject is so strange?

Once we shed light on the subject of invaders of dark spirits, you will agree that it is not so strange after all. Jesus demonstrated His power against the dark forces which He called "devil" throughout His ministry, and He demonstrated and taught how to deal with this.

Entities, Possessions and Spirits and Their Role In Sickness

Jesus realized the fact that many, many people are sick, many carry burdens and many live lives of

darkness and imperfection. The burden is not
their own but the shadow, the darkness, the presence of evil spirits, the presence of demonic spirits. Many of our brothers who have mental or
emotional illnesses carry some kind of demonic
spirits. That is not enough. Up to a third of all
physical ailments are involved in spiritual, dark,
destructive powers which we cannot see. Once
these dark forces are removed, the body can re-
cuperate, sometimes instantly, sometimes in
hours, days or weeks.

Jesus knew about these dark forces and
called them out by name. He healed the people
sometimes by laying on of hands, sometimes by
His divine spoken word, always demanding
Satan to "go behind."

I want to make sure that you remember the
words, "This and more thou shall do in my
name." In order to clarify my point, *the tremendous influence of evil spirits as a contributing factor to ill health* has to be known. We have to
know about these things.

Many illnesses have a dark side. When the
dark forces are lifted out, the people are healed.
And Jesus healed them all. No one has the
power as Jesus had, but we could, we should realize that a quarter to a third of all physical illnesses have a destructive power of a dark spirit
in it and once we release this, automatically the
illness can be healed. I want to make you aware
that the triumph of that foe is, that most people
think the spirit of darkness does not exist.

Therefore, the foe can enter like a thief in the night. He can enter your house, your aura because you let the doors open and this foe will give your body blow after blow and you don't know where it is coming from.

The days of triumph of the dark forces are those when mankind says, "There is no God. God is dead." That is when the "devil" gains power over us and over nations.

The Bible teaches the existence of the dark forces. It is one of the seven spiritual causes of illnesses and it is the biggest and most powerful force. The forces that battle the light, we have to know more about them, we have to know the truth.

Obsessive Powers Causing Mental Illness

This illness is growing in leaps and bounds not only in our country but all over the world. Schizophrenia is split mindedness. Suddenly the person can change into someone else. Most of them become violent at times for an hour or less or for days or even months. Most of them do not know that their behavior was so destructive that they had to be put in a hospital and under tranquilization.

Paranoia

A paranoid person thinks that someone is against him, that someone is plotting against him, that someone is tapping his telephone or that someone evil follows him. This last attitude is the clue. Truly a demonic force is behind or with him sending dark energy.

Depression

Depression is very, very often of physical origin, as with *Candida albicans*, low blood sugar or chemical and environmental poisons. In these mentioned diseases which weaken the defense system of the body, dark forces may leak into the body spirit and make matters worse.

Suicide

Demons can take hold of these tortured brothers. These vicious forces can overcome the divine will to live and instruct a person to jump out the window, take the sleeping pills, the poison is good for you, the bullet is the answer to your depression.

Alcoholism

True alcoholism is not only *Candida albicans* lodged in the liver, but also a blue demon looking over the left shoulder of someone affected with this trouble. This demon will say: "drink, it is harmless, drink, no one knows it, drink, it will relax you," and the blue demon wins.

Drugs and Lust

These are tools of dark forces. They are tools of demonic entities which want to make their dark appearance in the physical body. They suppress the spirit body of light and take over.

Spastic Entities

We deal with spastic entities. These are forces which keep a muscle or a group of muscles in constant tension. I have seen people who have to hold their heads to the right or to the left. Painful and frightening. I have seen people who cannot open one hand as if in constant spasm. Some drag their feet and some have spasms on others areas of the body. It can be permanent or it can appear only at times. This is very difficult to deal with.

Mental Entities

There is one more dark force to be mentioned. That is a force which invades our mental realm. It is like a heaviness over our head and over our thinking and we are hindered to make a clear decision in any matter. When we make a decision, we cannot stick to it. These mental spooks are a great deal with our young people. Boys and girls sway back and forth in college. One semester they take art (basket weaving), and the next semester they take engineering just to go back to an easier subject. These mental entities like to have the driver's seat. They are not satisfied to play a second role as in obsession or as the spastic entities just occupying a set of muscles. Mental entities want to direct a person in behavior and in purpose in life or, let us say, lack of purpose in life and foresight.

Once we have understood that there is more than our eyes can see, once we have learned that these invasive powers are for real, all efforts should be made

    A. to learn more about them,
    B. to learn how to eliminate them, and
    C. how to stay clear from them.

It always was the task of the priest, the task of the churches to clear the demonic power, to leave the veil of darkness from the afflicted parishioners. Not anymore. It is considered old women's tales, it is not fashionable any longer. Strange to report that it is forbidden to the priest of some congregations to exorcise the afflicted.

We are in a time of "do it yourself," in a time where "God Helps Those Who Help Themselves." We have to be firm and look at our master Jesus and how he did it. Remember, He said "This and more thou shall do in my name." Being in His name means doing His work and to do His work you let Jesus our Lord work through you. There is a mystical spirit and a tremendous power of light in the name of Jesus. It is the person against the dark foe, against demonic forces, against our common enemy, the devil.

How To Take Care of Evil Imps

I was invited to speak in Cleveland, Ohio at Bishop Gilbert's church. The meeting hall was in a huge old mansion with fifteen bedrooms, huge stairways, beautiful old stained glass windows, wood carvings and high ceilings.

At night, a bed was made in one of the bedrooms. It had a bath attached to it and was a cozy atmosphere. I was all alone in this tremendous dwelling. I had shut off the lights and had finished my prayers, when a tremendous turmoil was outside my door, in the bathroom, yes, in the entire house.

I got up and blessed the doors and windows with my cross and told the imps that I didn't want them here. The turmoil went on. So I opened the door just a little and said, "In Jesus' name I command that you are quiet now. I am tired, I want to sleep. You may wake me up tomorrow morning at 5 a.m." It was quiet all night. I slept like a baby.

Five minutes to five, I woke up. It was quiet and I thought, "I wonder what the imps are up to." Exactly at 5 a.m., a terrible noise of screams and pounding of shouting and shrieking filled the air. I opened the door and said "Okay, guys, I heard you. Thanks for letting me sleep. Now stay quiet. I have to get dressed and pray."

They quieted down to an occasional whisper and I could sit down and meditate and study. These were house guests often found in old mansions; you call them spooks or ghosts. I don't know what they are, but I know that they obey the spoken word. They obey the word of Jesus.

How To Take Care of Mental Entities

In my opinion, forces of darkness that hover over a person and pull them from their goal are the easiest to take care of.

I mean these dark brothers who obstruct the vision and future of our young people. This is the way to do it. Light a candle and set it on a table. Have your brother, in need of deliverance, stand in front of the table. Pull your right little finger, thumb and middle finger into the palm of your hand so only two fingers stand up.

Place your left hand on the left shoulder of your brother. Start at bottom with one finger on each side of the spine and slowly move up. When you arrive at the top, draw your right hand under the left hand and both hands go down over the arms. Shake your hands and start again. Do this several times and while doing it say, "In the Name of Jesus, I deliver you from the dark forces which are over you and obscure your mental vision." After you have done this five to seven times, demand the dark forces to go through the candle light into the real light, so that they are made pure and free.

Earthbound Spirits

Dr. Edith Fiore writes, "Many people are possessed by earthbound spirits." She stated that eighty percent of her clients are possessed or obsessed. The symptoms range from mild to severe, such that people have to be hospitalized or even institutionalized.

Dr. Fiore advised to work on yourself and watch for the following symptoms:

- Low energy levels
- Character shifts
- Mood swings
- Inner voices speaking
- Impulsive behavior
- Poor concentration
- Sudden onset of anxiety
- Sudden onset of depression
- Weight gain without reasons

Dr. Fiore has delivered over a thousand people from possession. She said you can do it yourself. Talk to the spirit and tell it to leave. Tell this earthbound spirit that there is a world of light without sickness or pain. Tell the earthbound spirit to go in peace.

And Jesus said to His Disciples, "This kind (entity) does not go out except through fasting and prayer."

What happens in fasting is this: The body goes to work upon the wastes stored in the system and starts to eliminate the debris. A short fast dislodges the entities. It throws them off balance. Then it becomes easier to eliminate them. Jesus also said prayer. An honest prayer opens the door to the world of invisible helpers. Without these holy ones, we cannot do anything anyway.

Earthbound Entities

Many diseases are accompanied by earthbound entities. I remove them in the following way.

On a table, set six cinnamon scented candles. Use the short ones. Place a flat dish with the picture or saliva sample of the person to be delivered. Five inches away, set a dish of clear water. Make it full to the rim. In front of the dish with water, set a taller candle. This does not have to be scented. Sprinkle lightly with cinnamon powder. Take your cross and sweep over this altar setup I described. Say, "In Jesus' name, you earthbound ones go to the light, cleanse yourself in the water and go to the light. Jesus is showing you the way. Leave us alone and go." You take your own words and clear them out. Do the sweeping motion from the first candle over the picture over the water, leave the last tall candle. Repeat the saying about seven or nine or eleven times. If you have many pictures do it nine or eleven times in full faith and it will be done.

Removal of Spastic Entities

Spastic entities have their living quarters in the subcutaneous tissue. Often times, they occupy only one set of muscles, as the muscles in the neck (turning the head to the side). They may live in the muscles holding the spine, or anyplace involving muscles and spasticity. We look at diseases, such as epilepsy, spastic paralysis, cerebral palsy, some cases of hypertension, asthma or voice-shut-off. In all of these cases there may be an entity involved. We should look at these things with love.

Into this category of removing subtle invasions goes the excellent work of Dr. John Ray, called the Ray Method. Dr. Ray's main work and his terrific results stem from the fact that spastic entities can be released by holding certain trigger points on the body. It is a fascinating work.

The Power of Faith

Throughout the Bible, faith is stressed. Throughout any religion, faith is stressed. Religion without faith is unthinkable. *Faith* is an inner connection between you and the universe. *Faith is* the road between you and God. *Faith* is confidence in things unseen. We all have very little faith. Even Jesus said, "Oh, you with your little faith." Spastic entities are removed by *faith* and the spoken word.

Obsession in Blood, Caused by Transfusions

Dr. Dorothy Shepherd found that electronic tunings for obsession registered in the blood of individuals who had received transfusions or given blood to others, while individuals who had never given or received practically never exhibited any obsession in the bloodstream. Treating the obsession out of the bloodstream brought about a decided improvement in the physical and emotional welfare of the patient.

"Blood, as the vehicle of life, is specific to each individual, containing properties peculiar to each person; aggravations and conflicts, physical, mental and spiritual, are likely to ensue when foreign blood is introduced. We know not what the ultimate outcome will be, a total change of personality is likely. ... This is too long and serious a subject to be dealt with in a few short phrases."

The vibratory disharmony created by blood transfusions creates an attraction for obsessing entities, just as a diseased condition attracts entities. When this disharmony is in the bloodstream, the invading entities associate themselves with the blood, creating the particular condition designed by the author as obsession of the blood.

Garlic removes obsession in the blood.

The only published reference to this subject that is known to us occurs in the book _Homeopathy for the First-Aider,_ by Dr. Dorothy Shepherd, published by _Health Science Press of England._

Alcohol Demon (Blue Demon)

To remove the blue demon, obtain some holy water (or make it yourself). Obtain a bright red cloth the size of a handkerchief but fold it so that it has the thickness of a potholder. Let the person sit in a chair. Do it in a manner so that a door is nearby. Tell the person in question that you are going to remove the blue demon. Remove his/her clothes from the left shoulder. Now moisten the cloth with the holy water and ask for assistance from the angels. Plunge the so prepared cloth with one whoop over the shoulder and then escape through the nearby door. The reason for this escape is that, as the demon leaves, the person so treated jumps and chokes your throat. A few seconds later, they calm down.

Drug Related Entities

To remove drug related entities, you have to go to herbs. Give the addicted persons 2 caps of chaparral herb, 3 times daily for 10 days. Then prepare the following solutions. The following recipe comes from a famous healer from the Philippines.

Take 4 white pebbles from your back yard. Take your pendulum and check them out. Two pebbles should "gyrate your pendulum clockwise," 2 pebbles should "gyrate your pendulum counterclockwise." Wash them and simmer them in 1 quart of water for 20 to 30 minutes. Have the afflicted drink this water in one sitting. Since by boiling some of the water is evaporated, it is really only 3 cups they have to take. Some people throw up, some have diarrhea, some get the urge to walk and walk and have the urge to talk and talk. Whatever happens, don't be worried, the drug demon is leaving. Melilot, an herb, removes drug deposits.

Doctors are Baffled by Man's Death After Voodoo Curse

Cursed by voodoo, a 33-year-old Arkansas man died of heart failure in the hospital ... after days of living in terror.

Doctors could find no logical explanation for his death. "It was mystifying in that no medical illness was ever proven," said Dr. Roy Ragsdill, Jr., the psychiatrist who handled the bizarre case at the University of Arkansas Medical Sciences.

The uncanny death was revealed in the *American Journal of Psychiatry*. The victim, a black sawmill worker from a rural area north of Little Rock, AK, was admitted to the hospital when a nervous disorder was suspected.

"The patient had become increasingly irritable and withdrawn from his family," said Dr. Ragsdill. He was transferred to the psychiatric ward when his condition worsened.

"He became increasingly more agitated, confused and delirious. He began to have hallucinations and was terrified whenever people approached him. We put him on a high dosage of tranquilizers.

That's all we could do to slow him down. But we had to restrain him."

The patient's wife told doctors that her husband had angered a woman considered to be a witch. "He hadn't paid her for her services," said Dr. Ragsdill. "It was obvious they all believed in the stuff [voodoo] and that it was very real. He could never tell us why he'd been cursed. He never really communicated at all."

The man had had no previous history of any psychiatric disorder, Dr. Ragsdill told *The Enquirer.* "To the best of my knowledge, it developed after the hex was put on him.

"After two weeks in the hospital, the patient suffered a cardiac arrest. All efforts to revive him failed. He had no history of cardiovascular disease and an autopsy provided no reason for his death.

"But this is a pattern that is reported in the medical literature of patients said to have been cursed or put under a voodoo hex. I wouldn't be surprised if that were not the main reason for this man's death."

Why does voodoo work? "If you believe in it, a voodoo hex can have impact on you," said Dr. David C. Tinling, in charge of the psychiatric consultation service and associate professor in the department of psychiatry at the University of Rochester Medical Center, Rochester, NY.

"The belief in it is all-important. We think it leads to some profound shifts in the autonomic nervous system—your inner regulating system that takes care of your vital functions."

Spirits—both good and bad—invade the minds and bodies of people who are considered mad, says a clinical psychologist.

"I have treated mental patients whose minds had been taken over by spirits," said Dr. Wilson Van Dusen. "I have examined thousands of patients and I believe these spirits were present in every single one."

Not all spirits are evil. Dr. Van Dusen said he discovered a higher order of spirits with dazzling abilities and knowledge which seemed to help and protect the patient.

Dr. Van Dusen, Ph.D., who was chief psychologist at Mendocino State Hospital in California for 12 years, said he has communicated with some of the spirits.

"Whenever the voice of the spirit stated, I asked the spirit questions and the spirit would give me the reply through the patient."

The evil spirits seemed to possess people who had violated their own conscience, he said.

These spirits often inflicted pain and plotted ways to kill the person they possessed, torturing the victim with threats and obscene suggestions, he added.

"Most patients reported voices that told them they were worthless and should be killed."

But Dr. Van Dusen also found kind spirits of a higher order—apparent angels that acted with great respect for the patient.

Dr. Van Dusen, who was also former associate professor of psychology at John F. Kennedy University in Orinda, CA and author of several books and dozens of scientific papers on his research, said, "It was very rarely" that he could "break through the spirits to cure a patient" through conventional psychotherapy.

"I had to go back into ancient literature on possession for help."

As I stated, a quarter to a third of all physical illnesses harbor a dark force in them. It is a terrible destructive power. Seventy-five percent of emotional and mental illnesses have their causes in this dark power which sometimes is of demonic nature. I say sometimes because demon possession is the worst and not everyone possessed or obsessed has a demonic entity.

The task of the churches is to watch over their flock so that demonic forces will not enter the homes or their congregation. And if by one or another reason they do enter, it is the task of the minister to try to release the darkness surrounding a person, an illness or a situation. I say to try, because only Jesus could heal them all.

Unfortunately, this task of protection is not exercised any longer and the big foe has plenty of room to expand. Thank God we have a few preachers who dare to speak up. In their tent meetings and wonderful, healing "release meetings" many are freed from satanic, demonic and other lower forces which found entrance into their protective shield, the aura.

Many psychologists are now of the firm opinion that some of their patients may be possessed. These doctors are realizing that the devil does have power on this earth. They also realize that they have to unite with priests or other experts who are capable of removing dark forces from their unfortunate fellow man. This brings us to the realization that we also have to protect ourselves daily from the influence of dark forces. Pope Paul VI stated that he was convinced that the devil was on the attack at every level of society.

Daily Protective Devices
Against Dark Forces

Ninety-two percent of all energy is in the unseen world, the unmanifested; only eight percent is manifested energy. This makes you aware that you have to have a protective device. I am using the Indian Wheel with the cross in the middle and also the Indian Wheel with the heart of Jesus in the middle.

Rev. Doris Gilmer gave me the following recipe:

1 part of sea salt
1 part sand
1 part cinnamon
1 part sulfur

Put this in a small bag and carry it with you.

The American Indians cleanse themselves from dark forces by burning sage and cedar in their worship and homes.

Eucalyptus oil has a very profound protection against these scavengers.

Mount a mirror on the entrance of your home so that the incoming visitors can see into it. Accompanying earthbound spirits cannot come in. They have to wait outside. Place over the house door the ninety-first Psalm.

Take a plate full of sea salt. Hold it in your left hand and bless the salt with your right hand. Then throw a pinch of this blessed salt into every corner of your dwelling.

Against Entities Earthbound

4 parts   asafoetida
3 parts   lobelia
12 parts   spikenard
5½ parts cayenne

Carry this with you.

For mental health take sage, sesame and hazelnut. It makes you immune to psychic attack.

Emotional Entities

8 parts   valerian
8 parts   wild yam root
8 parts   blue cohosh
6 parts   anise seed
6 parts   ginger

Make tea. Drink 2 cups a day.

Emotional Entities

4 parts   spikenard
8 parts   carrot seed
10 parts   black walnut leaves
5 parts   red poppy flower
6 parts   marigold

Mind Tonic

2 oz   cyany flower
2 oz   chamomile
2 oz   rose petal
2 oz   orange blossom
2 oz   spearmint

CHAPTER VII

You Can Heal

When nothing can be done about a problem, we've overlooked something.

—*Mark Walters*

I asked Rev. Dr. Fred Houston one day, "Why did we come to experience this earth's life?" He answered, "To learn the truth. To know and learn the truth is the most important task in our life. All experiences in life are needed to find the truth and 'the truth' will make us free."

This is what you do! Every morning, give yourself a treat, just a little treat. Say to yourself, "Yesterday, I failed here or there, but today I am under 'New Management' and I start anew." I personally add Luke 1:37, "For with God nothing shall be impossible."

The Power of the Spoken Word

The power center of the spoken word is the throat center. Sound is a creative energy.

- Can Create
- Can Destroy

If the spoken word has power, it has to have enthusiasm. The sound of the spoken word affects the thyroid gland, then the thymus gland and then the spleen. The thyroid, thymus and spleen are then the center of the immune system. Therefore, the spoken word is a constructive rebuilder.

The wave of the spoken word goes on to the pineal gland, stimulating it; then to the pituitary gland, balancing it. Then on to the saliva glands, the solar plexus and the adrenal glands. Every center in our body is affected by our speech. It intensifies the aura or dissipates the aura.

The power of the spoken word is not only for yourself, it also is for others. Every time we speak, we send out sounds through our etheric, astral and mental centers.

This is the mechanical way a spoken word goes. On its way to the aura it stimulates all glands or depresses all glands. The spoken word uplifts or destroys.

When a physician tells someone, "You have only three weeks to live," the glands close up. The immune system closes up. No help is available to restore the health.

The Bible says, "And whatsoever ye shall ask in my name that will I do." All life is vibration. If we are vibrating on injustice and resentment, we will meet it on our pathway, at every turn.

To change your mood, you must change your vibration. I say, change your words and you will change your vibration. You are a master workman and your tools are your words. Be sure you work constructively. According to the divine plan, man is a distributor of God power. Man does not create this force, but man was given the power, the vibration of this power of God. Man has power and dominion over the elements. Jesus said, "Rebuke wind and waves."

We should be able to set an end to drought, an end to war and an end to epidemics. How? Through the power of the spoken word.

Science and religion are now coming together. Science is discovering the power within the atom. Religion (in advanced understanding) teaches the powers within—*thoughts and words. Speak the power of healing and the chemistry in man changes. An inexhaustible energy in man is released by good will through the power of the spoken word. A man free from fear could say to the mountain of hate and war, "Be thou removed," and they would return to nothingness.*

On this page, I have to bring your attention to a new branch of science, the *Bio-electrical-chemistry* of the body.

Dr. Seeger Berlin found that cell life can turn right or left. This right or left turning inside the very cell can be measured with a polarimeter. Dr. Seeger and Prof. Warburg call it cell respiration. Prof. Warburg and others said, "When there are electrobiochemical disturbances in the cell, so that the cells cannot form their natural cycles of positive and negative electrical charges, all carbohydrates will then produce negative D cells.

Cell Respiration

Milk cyclone fermentation can have D-positive or D-negative aspects in the living cell. Scientists call it milk cyclone D-positive and D-negative.

The prolonged left turning cycle of D-negative milk ferment is a cause of cell deterioration. It is stopping cell respiration so that the cell nucleus forms its own entity cancer.

Dr. Engelhardt demonstrated that the heart muscle can only use D-positive milk cyclone for its electrochemical balance and strength. It is obvious that other muscles require the same for maintenance and repair. The skin is particularly thankful to D-positive foods.

D-positive milk cyclone activates the lymphatic system and detoxifies the entire body from environmental and other poisons.

What can we do to improve our defense system? What can we do to assume that D-positive milk cyclone is formed? Every culture, every nation has its own national drink or food which in one way or another is served in a fermented state.

It is the traditional yogurt of Bulgaria, Iran and Turkey, a daily drink made from yogurt and thinned down with spring water—it is the kefir. It is also the sauerkraut in Germany, the raw fish in Scandinavia, the fermented drink in South America and on and on.

We can have it all but, because of lack of knowledge, very few of us use a fermented food or drink every day.

One of the richest foods in D-positive terms is beets. Red beets are the queen of all. Just 1 tsp. of beet powder will suffice. A soup with red beets or relish made out of beets will turn the cell to D-positive. It also is a detoxifier of environmental poisons.

We had the impression that it is the color in beets which prevents metastasis in cancer but, through the biochemical and electrobiochemical works of researchers, we find that it is the positive influences of beets to the D-negative cell that makes the miracles.

True prayers can turn the D-negative biochemical, electrochemical stream into D-positive expression and instant healing will result.

We live in a stressful world. What can we do to stay sound?

1. Examine your problem.
2. Singing in groups in churches or by yourself reduces and releases stress.
3. Recite a poem.
4. Physical exercises help tremendously.
5. Look at a problem with a humorous outlook. In every problem is something funny.

6. A belief in something sacred, holy, in these things that stimulate happiness and thankfulness.

Learning to Open Pineal And Pituitary Glands

The pineal gland is the door to God's grace. After bad news, after death of your beloved one, the pineal closes.

Take both hands, fingers up, palms together. Open your hands several times and ask that the pineal will be opened and divine power will flow in. This is very important.

To open the pituitary gland (which is the seat of will power) is more difficult.

Opening the Pituitary Gland With Crystal Healing

Crystal healing is practiced all over the world. Crystals accumulate divine power and give it off by command. The most important and most neglected part in this type of healing is that a crystal has to be cleansed before it is used for healing. The crystal will hold on to the vibration it was used on before. For example, if one used a crystal to bring healing to a skin problem, this problem would jump to the crystal and has to be cleared.

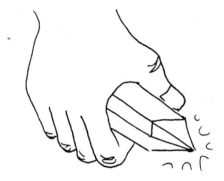

A crystal has to be put in salt or saltwater for at least five minutes to be cleansed. Then give your demand of healing, and your demand is multiplied many times in the crystal.

Healing the pituitary is most important. This gland is resting on four spiritual columns. In order to have lasting results, do the following:

Take a purified crystal. Invoke the healing demand as, "please heal this pituitary now." Hold crystal in your right hand and point with crystal to the first 4 points indicated on the head in the diagram below. On each one you demand that this column will be strong and uphold the pitu-

Points to Touch with the Crystal

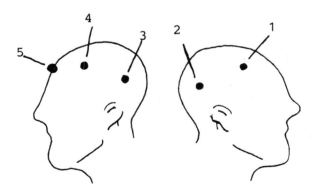

itary. After you have touched the first 4 points, you touch point 5, the forehead where the hair starts (or used to start), and also demand that the pituitary will be opened, and it will be opened and stay open!

Place the crystal back into the salt or salt water.

As soon as the pituitary is working your prayer has tremendous power. It flows through your hands. Hold your hands together as in the picture below. Let the palms open. With this you have an instrument to heal. It is far beyond your wildest dreams. Put it over a sick person, over a picture of someone in need, or perhaps over the map of our country and watch miracles of healing happen.

Synchronizing the Brain

After you have balanced your light centers, synchronize your brain. Your brain is your control tower. It has to be in balance. Take a crystal in your left hand. The crystal should not be cut, one side being rough. A crystal is a tool which multiplies your thoughts many times.

Talk to the crystal: "I will that you become an instrument of our Lord, that you help to balance this person's brain and pituitary gland."

Referring to the diagram above, take each section of the brain and say, "In the name of the Most High, be balanced!" Go from section to section, no. 5 is last. Every time ask for balance. Now you are in balance. Now you are ready to heal others. Give thanks to our Lord.

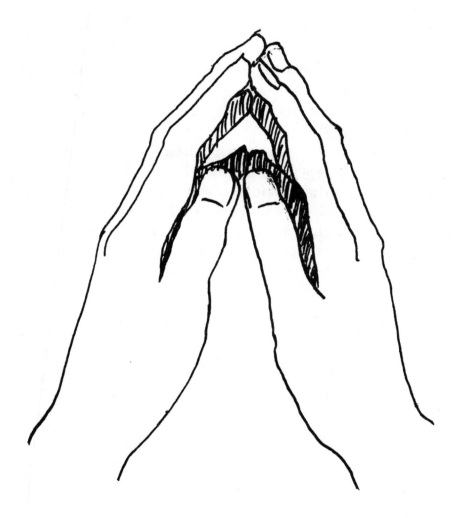

When the pituitary and pineal glands are open, your hands become a healing instrument.

Ten Commandments for Maintaining Perfect Health

Cause is in subconsciousness—the unseen.
Effect is in circumstances—the seen.

1. Accept criticism as the other person's problem, not yours.

2. Appreciate yourself and reaffirm your self-worth whenever necessary.

3. See the good points in circumstances. See even problems as happening for the best.

4. Rather than looking backward with sorrow, look forward with joyous expectation.

5. Rather than fretting about what you do not have, appreciate what you have.

6. Learn from mistakes so that you can convert them into triumphs.

7. Insulate yourself from distasteful surroundings through wholesome detachment.

8. Let go readily of what you no longer need and make the most of what you now attract.

9. Grow in courage and self-mastery from every circumstance.

10. Be aware of the larger consciousness of which you are a part.

These might be called the ten commandments to good health. They are beyond the physical—in the unseen world of consciousness.
Observe them and enjoy perfect health.
Positively.

Books by Hanna

"Wholistic health represents an attitude toward well being which recognizes that we are not just a collection of mechanical parts, but an integrated system which is physical, mental, social and spiritual."

Ageless Remedies from Mother's Kitchen

You will laugh and be amazed at all that you can do in your own pharmacy, the kitchen. These time tested treasures are in an easy to read, cross referenced guide. (92 pages)

Allergy Baking Recipes

Easy and tasty recipes for cookies, cakes, muffins, pancakes, breads and pie crusts. Includes wheat free recipes, egg and milk free recipes (and combinations thereof) and egg and milk substitutes. (46 pages)

Alzheimer's Science and God

This little booklet provides a closer look at this disease and presents Hanna's unique, religious perspectives on Alzheimer's disease. (15 pages)

Arteriosclerosis and Herbal Chelation

A booklet containing information on Arteriosclerosis causes, symptoms and herbal remedies. An introduction to the product *Circu Flow*. (14 pages)

Cancer: Traditional and New Concepts

A fascinating and extremely valuable collection of theories, tests, herbal formulas and special information pertaining to many facets of this dreaded disease. (65 pages)

Cookbook for Electro-Chemical Energies

The opening of this book describes basic principles of healthy eating along with some fascinating facts you may not have heard before. The rest of this book is loaded with delicious, healthy recipes. A great value. (106 pages)

God Helps Those Who Help Themselves

This work is a beautifully comprehensive description of the seven basic physical causes of disease. It is wholistic information as we need it now. A truly valuable volume. (196 pages)

Good Health Through Special Diets

This book shows detailed outlines of different diets for different needs. Dr. Reidlin, M.D. said, "The road to health goes through the kitchen not through the drug store," and that's what this book is all about. (90 pages)

Hanna's Workshop

A workbook that brings together all of the tools for applying Hanna's testing methods. Designed with 60 templates that enable immediate results.

How to Counteract Environmental Poisons

A wonderful collection of notes and information gleaned from many years of Hanna's teachings. This concise and valuable book discusses many toxic materials in our environment and shows you how to protect yourself from them. It also presents Hanna's insights on how to protect yourself, your family and your community from spiritual dangers. (53 pages)

Instant Herbal Locator

This is the herbal book for the do-it-yourself person. This book is an easy cross referenced guide listing complaints and the herbs that do the job. Very helpful to have on hand. (109 pages)

Instant Vitamin-Mineral Locator

A handy, comprehensive guide to the nutritive values of vitamins and minerals. Used to determine bodily deficiencies of these essential elements and combinations thereof, and what to do about these deficiencies. According to your symptoms, locate your vitamin and mineral needs. A very helpful guide. (55 pages)

New Book on Healing

A useful reference book full of herbal, vitamin, food, homeopathic and massage suggestions for many common health difficulties. This book is up-to-date with Hanna's work on current health issues. (155 pages)

New Dimensions in Healing Yourself

The consummate collection of Hanna's teachings. An unequated volume that compliments all of her other books as well as her years of teaching. (150 pages)

Old-Time Remedies for Modern Ailments

A collection of natural remedies from Eastern and Western cultures. There are 20 fast cleansing methods and many ways to rebuild your health. A health classic. (105 pages)

Parasites: The Enemy Within

A compilation of years of Hanna's studies with parasites. A rare treasure and one of the efforts to expose the truths that face us every day. (62 pages)

The Pendulum, the Bible and Your Survival

A guide booklet for learning to use a pendulum. Explains various aspects of energies, vibrations and forces. (22 pages)

Spices to the Rescue

This is a great resource for how our culinary spices can enrich our health and offer first aid from our kitchen. Filled with insightful historical references. (64 pages)